T0169192

COVID UNMASKED
A SURVIVOR'S GUIDE

by Tony Aspler
Illustrations by Calum Csunyoscka

**Even in desperate times there is always chocolate...
...and of course wine.**

mosaicPRESS

Library and Archives Canada Cataloguing in Publication

Title: COVID unmasked : a survival guide / Tony Aspler.

Names: Aspler, Tony, 1939- author.

Identifiers: Canadiana (print) 20200411217 | Canadiana (ebook) 20200411292 | ISBN 9781771615488 (softcover) | ISBN 9781771615495 (PDF) | ISBN 9781771615501 (EPUB) | ISBN 9781771615518 (Kindle)

Subjects: LCSH: COVID-19 (Disease)—Humor. | LCSH: COVID-19 (Disease)—Popular works. | LCSH: Epidemics—Humor. | LCSH: Epidemics—Popular works.

Classification: LCC RA644.C67 A87 2020 | DDC 362.1962/414—dc23

Published by Mosaic Press, Oakville, Ontario, Canada, 2020.

MOSAIC PRESS, Publishers
Copyright © Tony Aspler, 2020
Printed and bound in Canada.

Illustrations by Calum Csunyoscka©
Designed by Andrea Tempesta • www.flickr.com/photos/andreatempesta
Cover photo by Erik Mclean on Unsplash

ONTARIO ARTS COUNCIL
CONSEIL DES ARTS DE L'ONTARIO
an Ontario government agency
un organisme du gouvernement de l'Ontario

We acknowledge the Ontario Arts Council
for their support of our publishing program

Funded by the Government of Canada
Financé par le gouvernement du Canada

Canada

Mosaic Press acknowledges the support of Ontario Creates

MOSAIC PRESS 1252 Speers Road, Units 1 & 2, Oakville, Ontario, L6L 5N9
(905) 825-2130 • info@mosaic-press.com • www.mosaic-press.com

This book is dedicated
to my good friend, Gordon Pape,
who pressed me to do it.

Table of Contents

Introduction

A humorous booklet about COVID-19!

Why?

Because humour is our best ally in the fight against adversity.

A smile is a shaft of light and we need smiles to lighten the dark days as we, as a global community, are experiencing.

If we can smile and even laugh at the virus then this is a small, daily victory.

We are not giving into The Beast.

We are surviving.

We are accepting that this is a passage through which we must navigate, albeit a treacherous and culture-changing passage; and we need all the light and love we can get to guide us through.

I hope the following words will bring a smile to your face and make you forget for a moment the world's anxiety and loss.

Be safe and flourish (and treat yourself to a glass of wine.).

Cheers!

Proceeds from the sale of this book will be donated to Grapes for Humanity (www.grapesforhumanity.com)

A Passive-Aggressive Guide To Social Distancing

Here are some helpful hints to keep you safe when venturing out in public.

1. Do not bathe.
2. Instead of gum, chew garlic buds (carry a stash with you and offer them to strangers.)
3. Extend your palm to passers-by, inviting them to choose a card from your imaginary deck.
4. Acquire a shabby raincoat and flash your colostomy bag.
5. Tattoo your forehead with the words, 'Advertise Here.'
6. Paint a toothbrush black. Hold it under your nostrils. Raise your right arm and shout, 'Sieg Heil!'. (Repeat three times to ensure your audience has heard you.)
7. Use your index finger to beckon people closer — but remain silent while doing this. And always smile; look friendly.
8. If in doubt as to the efficacy of any of these instructions, talk to your psychiatrist. (If he/she will not listen to you, speak to your wife.)
9. Stay safe. We have your back. We're all in this together.

_____

_____

_____

_____

_____

(Fill in the blanks with any other cliché you can think of.)

While it might be the most effective way of keeping people at a distance, do not leave home with an assault weapon slung over your shoulder. Or worse, resist the urge to strap on a facsimile of a suicide vest. Trust me, you'll be arrested after ten paces and suffer a different kind of incarceration.

With regard to the wearing of masks, heed the words of Canada's Prime Minister Justin Trudeau: *'[A mask] protects others more than it protects you, It prevents you from breathing or speaking moistly on them.'* Needless to say, as soon as the words were out of his mouth, he regretted them. 'Speaking moistly' has now become a Canadian meme.

About Face

We are hearing all kinds of directives on radio, television and in print from the health authorities regarding how we should be combating COVID-19.

One such instruction is that we should not touch our faces. Unfortunately, my hearing is not as acute as it once was and I heard this as, 'Don't touch your feces' — which is good advice, virus or no virus. It's only human, however, to touch one's face to show emotion. Think of Edvard Munch's painting 'The Scream.' He'd be in deep trouble with the Face Police today, because I'm sure that they will begin to fine us if we're caught touching our faces in public.

What happens then if you get an itch? Well, I have the answer. Use your elbow; but make sure you haven't greeted anyone recently by knocking elbows. (Quick digression here: why should we knock elbows Instead of shaking hands when we're told to use our elbows to sneeze and cough into!)

By the way, if you can't reach your nose with your elbow, you have more to worry about than an itch.

In these difficult times I can understand why people will want to touch their faces. It's to confirm they still have one.

The second law of Nature is: If you have an itch it has to be scratched. How do you square this imperative with the need to protect yourself from yourself?

You have to do it remotely. That is, there is to be no skin-to-skin contact. Your kitchen drawer is full of medical equipment for the express purpose of relieving your itch. The longer the handle the better. Remember your grandmother's homily: 'He who sups with the Devil should have a long spoon.' Which means — the further you can keep your fingers from your face the better.

Smarten up people, practice your own bodily social distancing. Keep your hands to yourself. Sit on them if you feel an itch coming on and when the urge to touch your face becomes unbearable, meditate. Or lie down in a dark room with a wet flannel over your eyes.

If that does not solve the problem, fill the sink with warm water and immerse your face in it for ten minutes.

There will no longer be an itch to worry about.

Home Remedies For Covid-19

Forget it.

There are none.

No hot drink, no marijuana tea, no amount of tequila, no Vicks Vaporub, no garlic poultices — none of them will work.

What is under your kitchen sink is not a dispensary — whatever Dr. Trump might have suggested.

So, if you have the symptoms, call the doctor and let your next of kin know.

How To Actuate The Positive

This exercise has to do with psychology.

(A quick aside here: when my children were just impossible and needed disciplining, my then-wife said, 'Use Psychology on them.' So, I named a wooden spoon, 'Psychology.' It worked—till they left for university.)

In order to improve your mood, which will make you a more agreeable person to those locked down with you, think of COVID's silver lining:

1. With less traffic, the air you breathe—that gives you life—is purer
2. You can see fish in the Venice lagoons (if you can get there)
3. There are no car horns
4. People are politer to each other
5. Your nose will not be assailed by the body odours of others
6. There are no burglaries
7. No Jehovah's Witnesses will turn up on your doorstep
8. You can sleep in
9. No telephone offers of duct-cleaning. (Correction: I just had one)

As an exercise in Positive Thinking, add your own inspirational items to this list and magnetize them to the fridge door.

(Now, doesn't that make you feel better! Pour yourself a glass of wine. You deserve it. That's what I call 'Positive Reinforcement.' In the following chapters this will be abbreviated to **PR** to save space.)

Afterthought: Cover all the mirrors in your house, condo or apartment with towels — and hide the bathroom scale in the garage till the pandemic is over.

Home Schooling

With all the schools closed, your children are at home for many more exhausting hours than they used to be. But their education is of the greatest importance. (How are they going to support you in your old age if they don't get past Grade Five?)

So, they have to keep learning even if they don't have desks to sit at.

The first thing *you* as a parent will learn is that your kids are smarter than you are.

Just by watching them, you realise how comfortable they are in this Digital Age. Witness have they navigate on tablets and PC's, working the keyboards like young Mozart's.

Do not be dismayed by this revelation. The little buggers have only kept their over-all intelligence concealed from you in order to continue receiving pocket money – so they would not have to find a job commensurate with their intellectual abilities.

However, when it comes to on-line learning, it should not be too difficult to get them to sit in front of a television screen as this is the preferred default position for most kids.

Once they cotton on to the fact that they are being instructed rather

than entertained, this might come as a shock and there will, undoubt-
edly, be pushback. So, use some old-fashioned discipline technique,
such as bribing them with ice cream.

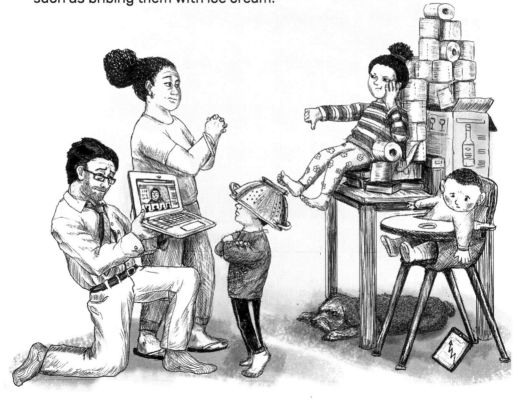

How To Keep Busy At Home

Here are some helpful suggestions as to what you might do to fill your day. (What you do at night is your own business.)

My Top 12 Time-filling Activities

1. Rearrange the spice drawer alphabetically (or by age if you are anal.).
2. Concoct a new perfume by pouring the remnants of fragrances and after-shave lotions into an empty wine bottle. (Remember to cork it and mark it well so that you don't accidentally consume it.)
3. Stencil inspirational messages on your living-room wall, such as: 'This Too Will Pass Before I do.'
4. Add up the number of screws in your tool box (separate the roundheads from the flatheads).
5. Write a daily letter of complaint to your MP (on whatever is bugging you at the moment).
6. Plan ahead for Christmas. Curate your Christmas list. Make decorations of the business cards you've accumulated over the years.

Make a Christmas wreath with all the corks that have mysteriously appeared in the kitchen wastebasket. This will make you feel good as you will be saving the planet. (If you need more corks, visit your local liquor store).

7.   Go through your EPs and tapes and search in the attic for something to play them on.
8.   Wind up the watches in the back of your bedside table.
9.   Sharpen all the lead pencils in the house.
10. Knit a face mask.
11. Change the batteries in the smoke detectors.
12. Teach yourself Mandarin.

(Just think of the sense of satisfaction you will receive by accomplishing the activities on this list. Treat yourself to a glass of wine. My neighbour Mark is building a car in his garage; I'm thinking of building an Ark — see final chapter.)

The Pontius Pilate Effect

How many times have you heard medical authorities instruct you to wash your hands?

We should be doing this, apparently, every three minutes.

If you find this tiresome, you can wash them once. However, the process should take two hours.

What else have you got to do anyway?

While you're washing your hands, pretend you're a surgeon on 'Grey's Anatomy'. This will make you feel better. Perhaps.

This hand-washing business doesn't mean you should neglect other parts of your anatomy.

Any exposed body part might come in contact with contaminated surfaces. Enough said.

What's an Essential Business?

At the onset of a pandemic, the government, in its wisdom, will designate which commercial enterprises, services and businesses are necessary to sustain the life of the population at large.

The rest will be ordered to close and shutter until such time as the government feels it is safe to gather taxes again.

If you own a business or a corporation you have to ask yourself, 'Is what I do essential?'

This is not an existential question. There can only be one of two answers: Yes or No.

In the 'Yes' category are such enterprises and services as

Grocery Stores
Pharmacies
Liquor Stores
Wineries/Distilleries
Golf Courses
Marriage Counsellors

In the 'No' category are:

Taxidermists
Disc Jockeys
Glider instructors
Firework manufacturers
Flag-makers
Bingo
Party shops
Tattoo parlours
Accordion makers
Antique stores
Organised Crime...

(This a partial list. I am leaving space for you to pencil in your own examples. If necessary, use more sheets of paper. But don't write on both sides of the paper at once. There are no wrong answers.)

How To Get Your Daily Exercise

When you are in lockdown in your house it is vital that you exercise each day to keep muscle tone.

Remember, you cannot burn calories on the couch — or on both ends — unless you are engaging in coitus.

I have devised a simple set of daily exercises to keep you fit while in captivity.

Every morning before breakfast, strip the bed and turn your mattress over. Not only will this exercise strengthen your arm and leg muscles as well as your core, but it will take up at least fifteen minutes of the day. Because you will have to unmake the bed, turn the mattress over and then make the bed again. To alleviate the boredom of this routine, sing a sea shanty as you work (as long as it isn't, 'Blow the Man Down.') To add interest to what might become a mundane and boring activity after a few weeks, give yourself an incentive: time yourself with a stop watch and log the results. If you beat your 'Best Performance' time, treat yourself to a glass of wine. **PR**.

Another exercise that is good for the arms and back is to carry a blue box full of empty wine bottles to the curb. But be sure to bring them

back to the house because you can augment your supply of toilet paper by soaking off the labels. (And also hide your consumption from the neighbours.)

If you miss your visits to the gym, this may not be a bad thing for your over-all well-being. I offer my own experience as a cautionary tale.

Three months shy of my 80th birthday I joined a gym.

The Institution — as I prefer to call it — rejoices in the name of 'Fit4Life.' The kind of name you might see on a car license plate.

I committed myself to a year's membership at my wife's behest, as she would like to have me around to do the heavy lifting — i.e. taking the garbage to the curb on Sundays (which, I pointed out, is meant to be a day of rest. But she responded that as I am Jewish, Sunday is not *my* day of rest.)

The Fit4Life gym is full of black mechanical devices that make the place look like a medieval torture chamber. Painted on the walls in two-foot high lowercase letters is the directive, 'no judgement.'

I'm not quite sure I understand the message. Does it mean I am meant to accept and absolve everything I observe here, or that the jury is still out?

Strategically placed on the walls around the gym are dispensers of putty-coloured paper and spritzer bottles of water. Members are enjoined to wipe down the equipment and the seat they have occupied with the wetted paper when they have finished.

I was obviously over-zealous in my use of the water bottle following a twenty-minute effort on a stationary bike as I was admonished by a young woman dressed head-to-toe in spandex. She tells me in no uncertain terms: 'You left the seat wet!'

A young man sports a red T-shirt with this legend on the front: 'Shut Up and Train.' But this does not stop people around him from jabbering away like game show hosts.

In fact, to alleviate the boredom of stretching and cycling and running, I eavesdrop unashamedly on conversations around me. I offer these verbatim examples: Two ladies of indeterminate age on neighbouring treadmills, are both wearing head phones and conversing loudly so they could communicate over the pounding music at disco decibels. 'The only good thing about ageing,' says one, 'is that you get closer to your IQ.'

Her friend replies: 'Passed mine years ago, dear. Shall we go for a beer after?'

And then there were the two gentlemen taking a breather in the free weights department:

'Was Jesus circumcised? It wasn't in the Commandments.'

'Of course, he was. Luke chapter 2, verse 21. He was Jewish, so he had to be. Eight days after his birth. I reckon the rabbi did it on New Year's Day, 01 then.'

'Wouldn't that be 02 because he was born on Christmas Day 01?' (I gave up listening after that.)

To enjoy the gym experience, you have to accept uncritically the total gym culture package. Black seems to be the sartorial colour of choice as if everyone is at the funeral of someone they didn't really care very much about, their presence an obligation rather than a tribute.

Everything worn here is tight fitting as if each article of clothing had been bought three sizes too small. And there is a special kind of slow, strutting walk practiced by young men in singlets that accentuates their musculature. It's almost in slow motion, an under-sea movement. Then there are those cycling gloves worn by muscle-bound men and exceptionally small women who loiter around the heavy barbells section.

The cycling gloves really freak me out because the sight of them takes me back to my public-school days in England. Every year the graduating Sixth Form was given a single lecture on sex education by a man of God whom we only knew as Canon Warner.

He was called in specially for this rite of passage.

Canon Warner wore gloves with the fingers cut off — like cycling gloves, only his were woolen. He wore them in the height of summer. Rather than lecture us on the birds and the bees, Canon Warner handed out paper and pencils and invited us to write down questions that we would like answered about sex. The thinking being, no doubt, that we might be too inhibited or embarrassed to stand and articulate our concerns about sexuality in front of our classmates.

These notes were folded in four and deposited in a whicker waste basket and then returned to the stage of the assembly room where Canon Warner held court.

He would pick one out, read it to himself and then crumple it up in disgust. If memory serves, he only answered in one in five of the questions submitted.

It had become an annual contest for sixth formers to gross-out the poor man with our anonymous questions about sex. Which may explain why many products of English public schools ultimately need psychiatric help.

In order to help those readers who would like to be initiated into the arcane mysteries of gymdom, I offer the following admonitions.

Do not work out next to someone who is wearing a belt large enough to grace the torso of a World Wrestling Federation champion. They could suffer a hernia at any moment from trying single-handedly to lift a Volkswagen above their heads. A burst blood vessel is not a pretty sight.

Do not stand between a man with tattoos and the mirror in which he's admiring himself while he does curls with 60lb weights.

Do not question why a woman would wear full make up to a gym. It has to do with the mating instinct.

Avert your eyes in the washroom when you see a grown man try to dry a letter he'd accidentally dropped in the urinal using the Dyson AirGlide.

And finally, under no circumstances smile. I have never seen anyone smile in a gym. Because keeping fit is a serious business.

Keeping Your Kids Amused All Day

It is essential to keep children busy when incarcerated at home otherwise they will start playing 'Doctor.'

Devise horizon-expanding games like, 'Hunt the Corkscrew'.

When they find it, treat yourself to a glass of wine. **PR**. (Make sure the hiding place is not too out of the way — say, under the living room couch or by your favourite armchair.)

To distract them should they begin to whimper about not being able to solve a simple Chess problem, dress yourself up in a bed sheet and leap out a closet as Casper the Friendly Ghost. This should have a calming effect.

Teach your children how to play Poker.

They're never too young to learn. But let them win at least one hand — unless you're playing for money and they've emptied the contents of their piggy bank on the table. Then all bets are off.

Prepare them for adult life by teaching them how to deal from the bottom of the deck.

And explain what a Trifecta is.

You can also sharpen their mathematical skills by challenging them to calculate odds. For example, if you put $10 on a horse with odds of 12 to 1, how much would they win if their horse came in first? (And how much would they give Daddy for taking you to the races?)

Invite your child to cut your hair (you will certainly deserve a glass of wine for that. **PR**.)

Or, to paint your toenails. But you get to choose the colour.

Play party games, like 'Guess What Day of the Week it Is!'

Guess how many bottles there are in your neighbour's Blue Box today.

Or 'Let's Tidy Up Your Room.'

Join The Maskerade

It is ironic, is it not, that banks now insist you wear a mask on entering their premises.
In the good old days (B.C.), you risked arrest if you went into a bank wearing a mask.
Now you are refused entry if you don't.

Here are some helpful hints on carrying off the obligation with panache and style.

1. If you have dentures you need not worry about a sudden dental malfunction. Masks act as safety nets for flying dentures. Or worst-case scenario, they become hammocks.
2. Masks conceal Botox lip botches.
3. Masks cover halitosis and garlic breath.
4. Masks improve your elocution by forcing you not to mumble.
5. If you have to approach the pitcher's mound, you no longer need to cover your mouth with your glove to prevent lip-readers stealing your signs.

6. Masks, if correctly worn, inhibit young children from picking their nose in public.
7. Designer masks can send instant social messages. You can choose your mood from a glut of emojis.
8. Masks can be used to telegraph your intentions. If, for instance, your mask has an image of a tongue hanging out, you're either Mick Jagger or you're on the way to your doctor.

Read My Mask

Then there are the masks with warnings, admonitions, and pleas for help. Examples:

'If you can read this, you're too close.'

'Can we uninstall 2020 and install it again? This version has a virus.'

'Every disaster movie starts with the government ignoring a scientist.'

'Calm down Karen. It's allergies.'

The internet is awash with masks of all designs, from the tasteful (Mona Lisa's smile covered with a mask) to the tasteless ('I used to cough to cover my farts. Now I fart to cover my coughs.')

Pets And Covid-19

Our dog of mixed breed, Rosie the Rescue, is finding this social distancing business very tiresome.

She comes from Texas and Texans are gregarious folk.

Dogs are pack animals by nature and Rosie is a two-pack-a-day gal.

In her own interest, I had to keep telling her, 'No sniffs, and definitely no butts.'

It is many years since Deborah and I had cats – two of them. Nancy and Tonia, were named after the figure skaters. (It turned out to be a self-fulfilling prophecy as Tonia would beat up on Nancy all the time). Thus, we had ample experience of feline behaviour and their aberrant psychology.

Cats are asymptomatic with inherent psycho-social tendencies. They are also scofflaws and immune to instruction. So, if you are owned by a cat, you have nothing to worry about.

If you catch your cat coughing, don't rush to take its temperature. It's probably just a hair ball.

Dogs, it seems, can contract COVID. Maci, a three-year-old Poodle Bichon living in Grimsby, Ontario, was the first canine in Canada to be affected. Apparently, she is healthy now after being subjected to tests in three orifices.

So, if you own a dog, don't let them French-kiss you. And social-distance from dogs not within your bubble.

On-Line Shopping

We, as a species, share the same mental foible. Tell us not to do some-thing and we will find a way to do it — and to justify doing it after the fact. Since the shops are closed (except for essential businesses) we have to satisfy the urge to shop by any process possible — which means resorting to on-line shopping.

Through Instagram, we fall prey to the blandishments of the adver-tisers and their siren call to purchase (in my case) a power washer — a device I never thought I needed until they showed how, magically, it cleaned the floor of what looked like a pigsty or maybe it was a fra-ternity house. (My wife has told me to stop buying Instagram stuff on-line, but the habit is hard to break.)

Although, together we watched a film on Instagram of a company in China that manufactures a cast iron skillet that is non-stick. They showed how the iron was melted at the temperature of the sun; and how it was polished and honed to a non-stick surface like HRH's Rolls Royce. (No bird poop sticks to that jalopy.)

I was all prepared to buy both sizes of the skillet when my wife said, 'Let's read the comments.' One of them said, the purchaser had ordered the two sizes only to receive two frying pans made of aluminum. *O tempora, O mores*.

Cloistered at home, the craving to shop becomes the more intense. I imagine I am not alone in the pent-up frustration of thwarted consumerism.

Just think what will happen when this pandemic is pronounced over. The race to shopping malls will be like the start of the Boston Marathon.

Get Plenty Of Sleep

Sleep refreshes the body — and also helps to pass the time. Make sure you get lots of it. Whatever the hour of the day or night.

But here is a cautionary tale that began when my wife complained that I snore.

Ever forgiving in other aspects of our co-habitation, she decided to record me in the act.

She played it back while I was sleeping. She played it back in all its orchestral glory, thinking this might cure me.

But she says I broke into a two-part harmony.

She tried giving me left hooks and I woke up with bruises up my arm.

She said, "I thought you were dead. You stopped breathing."

I heard, "You stopped breeding."

"I was doing it in my sleep!" I exclaimed.

In the spirit of inquiry, I asked her that if I slept in the guest room and she could not hear me, was I actually snoring?

She told me I wasn't a tree and since the guest room was next to our bedroom that, yes, no walls would be thick enough.

It takes a certain amount of self-criticism to reach the conclusion that your wife might be right about: a) your snoring, and b) about the need to do something about your snoring. So, as the final submission of the snorer to the snoree, I agreed to go to a sleep clinic to be tested.

It was in the depths of a Toronto winter; the snow was deep on the ground and more was falling. I was told I could bring reading material. I brought along a stack of New Yorker magazines that had been piling up by my desk. (I dreaded going to the mail box in case another edition arrived to be added to the unread pile.)

The bedroom I was assigned to was like a room in the Bates Motel. The art on the wall was enough to give me nightmares – blackbirds with yellow eyes, although the caption read, "Moonlight over the Prairies."

The technician went to work on me. He placed suction caps with wires on my head and face. The wires were inserted into a box at my bedside that would transmit my brainwaves and my movements to the technician's screen.

I felt like Frankenstein's monster.

There were cameras on the walls. Shades of The Twilight Zone.

He told me to go to sleep now. He would be in the next room and if I needed anything, I just had to call out.

The idea of trying to fall asleep when you know someone is watching you – a stranger to boot – is a surefire trigger for insomnia.

It was 8 o'clock. Normally, I go to bed after 11.

The bed was like a rock pile. It was a twin. At home, my wife and I and our wheaten terrier (Pinot the Wonder Dog) share a king.

The sheets on this bed had a thread count of 13. I know. I counted them. I habitually sleep on my stomach in the shape of a swastika. Here, I was forced to sleep on my back, so I wouldn't dislodge a wire and electrocute myself.

I lay there in the gloom like a frozen mummy for two hours. Eyes wide shut, wishing I was home.

Then I had to pee.

I screamed a pathetic, "Help!"

The technician came in rubbing his eyes. He unplugged me from the machine. I had to go to the washroom with the wires dangling from my face. I was terrified I'd run into someone. Norman Bates, perhaps. Through the doors along the corridor I could hear a cacophony of my fellow inmates, sleeping peacefully and snoring blissfully like buzz saws. Surely, I was not as bad as that.

Having made it to the bathroom, I looked at myself in the mirror. Reflected back at me was the Addams family's Christmas tree.

I returned to my room to be rewired by the technician.

Eventually, miraculously, I fell into the shallowest of sleeps, waking up for the eighth time at 5 a.m., exhausted.

I unhooked myself from the machine, dressed and went into the control room. The technician was unaware of my presence.

He was asleep. Snoring.

I helped myself to coffee, making enough noise to ensure he would become aware of me but keeping a safe distance so that I wouldn't alarm him with all the hardware hanging from my face.

"Well," I said. "How did it go?"

"You'll get the report from the doctor," he replied.

A week later I was summoned to the doctor who told me that I had sleep apnea and I needed a CPAP machine.

I asked if I could get a second opinion.

"You can always take the test again," he said, "in case there was a false reading."

Go through that again! I'd rather have a root canal.

Eleven hundred dollars later, I was the reluctant owner of a device that blows air up your nose through a hose attached to a face mask that makes you look like a Second World War fighter pilot.

There is also a water chamber that fits into this contraption. If it malfunctions, you drown.

The first night I felt as if I had a cat sleeping on my face.

My wife said I didn't snore.

That was because I couldn't sleep.

The next night I substituted vodka for the distilled water.

I slept, but I was drunk by midnight and fell out of bed, terrifying Pinot who howled and woke up the neighbourhood.

But slowly, slowly I'm getting used to fighting the Battle of Britain every night. And next Halloween, I'll wear the mask when I answer the door.

If we ever have Hallowe'en again.

Looking To The Future

In anticipation of another pandemic or a recurrence of the one we're already in, think of what the experience of COVID-19 has taught us. It is advisable to take following precautions and stock up on these provisions while they are still available.

Acquire His and Her generators, and have them colour-coded. One should be, perhaps, pink, the other blue, to distinguish them. In anticipation of a sudden blackout, tie a ribbon to the handle of one of them as you do with your suitcase at the airport. (If the memory of past travel makes you well up – get a grip, man up.)

I am suggesting the following list of survival items for a family of four. (Augment if there are more members of your household – especially the wine.)

- 1200 rolls of toilet paper
- 10 bags of self-raising floor
- Case of wine red (in magnums)
- 60 x 12 rolls of paper toweling

- 100 boxes of Kleenex
- 10 sacks of basmati rice
- 40 flats of baked beans
- Case of wine (white in double magnums)
- 50 pounds of lean ground beef, frozen in 1lb Ziploc bags
- 2 sacks of coffee beans
- 1 sack All-Purpose flour
- A year's supply of dog food
- 4 x 1 kilo tins of caviar (Go ahead, spend the kids' inheritance.)
- A case of 750mL bottles of Fernet Branca
- 24 bottles of Advil Extra Strength
- Case of wine (Rosé)
- A gross of candles
- Six packets each of Energizer batteries — A, AA, AAA
- 15 bars of Lindt Milk Chocolate (large)
- A book on Semaphore signaling.
- Case of wine (sparkling in Jeroboams).

In order to protect your property against marauders, install a portcullis and drawbridge over a moat to be filled with piranhas and croc-

odiles. (During construction, post a notice regretting the inconvenience to Postal operatives

In addition, you can mount twin 57mm Bofors on the roof to deter aerial penetration; and as an added precaution you can string razor wire around the perimeter of the property.

To facilitate interaction with the public at large — when you have to leave the house — purchase on-line from NASA, gently-used unisex space suits complete with helmets.

And should you wish to have visitors ensure that they have acquired said gently-used unisex space suits from NASA, complete with helmets.

Interpreting The Regulations

Finally, some clarification on the lockdown laws.
(I'm indebted to my old friend in London, Bernard Silver, for making everything crystal clear. I was in the Boy Scouts in England with Bernard eons ago. Everything I know about life I learned in the Boy Scouts – except 'How To Pick Up Women In Bars.')

Here follows a Talmudic explication of the COVID Commandments.

1. You MUST NOT leave the house for any reason, but if you have a reason, you can leave the house.
2. Masks are useless at protecting you against the virus, but you may have to wear one because it can save lives, but they may not work, but they may be mandatory, but maybe not.
3. Shops are closed, except those shops that are open.
4. You must not go to work but you can get another job and go to work.
5. You should not go to the Doctor's or to the hospital unless you have to go there, unless you are too poorly to go there.
6. This virus can kill people, but don't be scared of it. It can only kill

those people who are vulnerable or those people who are not vulnerable. It's possible to contain and control it, sometimes, except that sometimes it actually leads to a global disaster.

7. Gloves won't help, but they can still help so wear them sometimes, or not.

8. STAY HOME, but it's important to go out.

9. There is no shortage of groceries in the supermarkets, but there are many things missing. Sometimes you won't need toilet rolls but you should buy some just in case you need some.

10. The virus has no effect on children except those children it affects.

11. Animals are not affected, but there was a cat that tested positive in Belgium in February when no one had been tested, plus a few tigers here and there...

12. Stay 2 meters away from tigers (see point 11).

13. You will have many symptoms if you get the virus, but you can also get symptoms without getting the virus, get the virus without having any symptoms or be contagious without having symptoms, or be non-contagious with symptoms... it's a sort of lucky/unlucky dip.

14. To help protect yourself you should eat well and exercise, but eat whatever you have on hand as it's better not to go to the shops, unless you need toilet paper or a fence panel.

15. It's important to get fresh air but don't go to parks but go for a walk. But don't sit down, except if you are old, but not for too long or if you are pregnant or if you're not old or pregnant but need to sit down. If you do sit down don't eat your picnic, unless you've had a long walk, which you are/aren't allowed to do if you're old or pregnant.

16. Don't visit old people but you have to take care of the old people and bring them food and medication.

17. If you are sick, you can go out when you are better but anyone else in your household can't go out when you are better unless they need to go out.

18. You can get restaurant food delivered to the house. These deliveries are safe. But groceries you bring back to your house have to be decontaminated outside for 3 hours including frozen pizza.

19. You can't see your older mother or grandmother, but they can take a taxi and meet an older taxi driver.

20. You are safe if you maintain the safe social distance when out

but you can't go out with friends or strangers at the safe social distance.

21. The virus remains active on different surfaces for two hours... or four hours... or six hours... I mean days, not hours. But it needs a damp environment. Or a cold environment that is warm and dry... in the air, as long as the air is not plastic.

22. Schools are closed so you need to home educate your children, unless you can send them to school because you're not at home. If you are at home you can home educate your children using various portals and virtual class rooms, unless you have poor internet, or more than one child and only one computer, or you are working from home. Baking cakes can be considered math, science or art. If you are home educating you can include household chores within their education. If you are home educating you can start drinking at 10am.

23. If you are not home educating children you can also start drinking at 10am.

24. The number of corona related deaths will be announced daily but we don't know how many people are infected as they are only testing those who are almost dead to find out if that's what they

will die of. The people who die of corona who aren't counted, won't or will be counted but maybe not.

25. We should stay in locked down until the virus stops infecting people but it will only stop infecting people if we all get infected; so it's important that we get infected and some don't get infected.

26. You can join your neighbours for a street party and turn your music up for an outside disco and your neighbours won't call the police. People in another street are allowed to call the police about your music whilst also having a party which you are allowed to call the police about.

27. No business will go down due to Coronavirus except those businesses that will go down due to Coronavirus.

Hope that makes things clearer for you.

The Aardwolves Were First On The Ark

(A contemporary fable for wine lovers of all ages)

Before the rains came, Captain Noah had already considered emigrating.

But his wife, Naamah, thought otherwise. She wanted to live in the family home where their three sons, Ham, Shem and Japheth were born.

'But what will you do, Noah, if and when life gets back to normal?'

'My dear, I can always go into ship building with the boys — or open a zoo.'

But in his mind, Noah told himself that 'God would provide,' and all he needed was a sign.

So, without a decision on the family future, Noah ordered the animals to board the Ark, two by two, in alphabetical order.

The Aardwolves were first up the gangplank because they jumped the queue and streaked ahead of the other animals.

Logically, Mr. and Mrs. Aardvark should have been first to board, followed by the Albatrosses, the Alligators and the Alpacas.

But the Aardwolves were very excited and just too impatient to wait in line, as they had never been on a boat before.

The Turtles and the Snails were, of course, the last to board. And the rain started just as they labored their way into the lower deck. The crew was already shutting the great gopher wood doors when they inched on board.

Naamah, worried about where all the animals would sleep. She couldn't put the Lambs next to the Tigers, the Rabbits next to the Boa constrictors, or the Mice next to the Cats — and where would they house the Giraffes?

'Don't worry, my dear,' said Noah. 'We will practice social distancing. The Ark has been beautifully designed by the architecture firm of Shem, Ham & Japheth… Our brilliant sons. They've quartered the giraffes where there's lots of room — on the poop deck.'

'Talking about that,' replied his wife. 'How will we keep the place clean?'

'Simple,' said Noah. 'The rains will wash the decks. You'll see… First of all, I have to hold a meeting of all the animals to explain how we will live together in harmony until the flood is over.'

'But what about the smell?' asked Naamah.

'If it gets too bad, we'll cover our noses with pieces of cloth,' replied Noah.

'I just don't know how we're going to manage all this with a crew of eight. And let's not forget, you're no spring chicken, husband. You're 600 years old.'

'Have faith, my dear wife,' said Noah. 'Listen to that rain. We'd better batten down the hatches.'

'I can hear the Hyenas laughing already,' said Naamah. 'It's going be a long cruise... And where will I hang the washing?'

'I have to go and organize a meeting for all our passengers,' said Noah, 'Get Shem to put up a clothesline.'

And Noah wandered off to find the Elephant.

'Mr. Elephant,' said Noah. 'I want you to speak to the animals for me. You are big and strong and they will listen to you. Especially those unruly Aardwolves who jumped the queue to get on board. Would you use your trumpet to call them all together, please? I will tell you what I want you to say.'

"Ok,' said the Elephant. 'Just let me know when.'

Noah covered his ears.

'Now.'

The Elephant lifted his great trunk and let out an ear-splitting blast which shivered the timbers of the Ark as it launched itself on the rising waters.

As soon as the animals were gathered together, Noah whispered his instructions for all the animals in the Elephant's large ear.

'We are all in this together,' repeated the Elephant, like a ventriloquist's dummy. 'We have your backs. It will be over in 40 days — according to my intelligence. So, I want you to be patient and live together in peace and harmony until the world returns to normal. That is, when the waters subside.'

'When that happens,' continued Noah, 'I will need a volunteer to leave the Ark on a reconnaissance mission — to make sure it's safe for us all to disembark.'

The Cows, hungry for fresh grass, were the first to put their hooves in the air; but Noah pretended he didn't see them. As we all know, Cows are not great swimmers and there would be lots of water about.

'We need someone who can fly over the land,' the Elephant said, when prompted by Noah.

The Vultures raised their wings, 'Pick us, pick us!' they shrieked.

But Noah knew that if the Vultures left the Ark, they would just eat everything they saw and never return.

'Where are the Doves?' asked Noah.

Before the Doves could be found, a wind of such force suddenly blew which created towering waves. The Ark bucked and heaved, sending the animals skittering across the decks, first to port and then to starboard, then back again.

This motion was particularly hard on the Flamingos with their long legs; and the Monkeys, feeling seasick, began to swing from the rafters.

The Parrots took flight and started screaming, 'We're all going to die! We're all going to die!'

At the helm, Ham, Noah's eldest son, had a hard time keeping the Ark on a steady course.

'Hold on tight,' yelled Ham to his brother, Japheth. 'There's going to be a second wave!'

The rolling of the Ark sent the Kangaroos hurdling over the Sheep and the Goats. The Ant-eaters hunkered down under a table looking for Ants. The Sloths slumbered in a corner.

'We need ballast,' shouted Noah. 'Take the hippopotami and the rhinoceroses down below. We have to steady the ship.'

Gradually the weather calmed but the rain kept falling. The Bulls gazed wistfully out of the port holes, watching the water rise and wondering if they would ever graze in pastures again.

Noah told the Elephant to announce to all the assembled animals that they should go to their allotted quarters where they would be given their dinner before bed...

And so, it came to pass that Noah's Ark sailed safely above the flood waters that submerged the cities of Sodom and Gomorrah — the Las Vegas and Reno of 2348 BC. The voyage lasted forty days and forty nights as Noah had predicted.

And on the fortieth day after the Ark had set sail, Noah awoke and saw that the storm had abated.

The sun was shining and the water was as calm as a mill pond.

He called to Naamah, 'Go and fetch the Dove, good wife. It's time for it to explore the land to see if it's safe for us to leave the Ark.'

Namaah went below to where the Doves were perched and carried the female back to Noah.

'Go forth and tell me what you see,' said Noah, releasing the Dove into the bright blue morning air.

By nightfall, the Dove had no returned and Noah was very sad thinking that the poor bird could not find land and was too tired to return to the Ark. He had no idea of what the future held for him.

He needed a sign.

He went to bed that night wondering if his family and the animals would ever leave the Ark.

Next morning, he was awoken by his son Ham's call from the quarter deck.

'Father, Father, come quickly. The Dove! The Dove, I see the Dove!'

Noah, his wife and his other sons rushed up to the quarter deck as the weary Dove landed awkwardly on the Ark.

In her beak she carried something that looked like a green leaf.

'It's a vine leaf!' exclaimed Noah. 'The waters have subsided! If the Dove could pluck a leaf from a grape vine, then the land must be free of water. It's a sign. I know what I have to do!'

The animals filed up from the decks below, two by two; and when the Elephant told them the news that they would soon be leaving the Ark, each one cheered in the only way they knew how.

Those with hooves and trotters pounded on the planks; those with talons and claws scratched at them; those with hard tails, like the Beavers, beat them on the deck; and the rest of the animals raised their voices in a cacophonous chorus of celebration.

The air was filled with quacks and cackles, bellows and roars, chirps and whistles.

And just then the first rainbow the world had ever seen arched over the sky — a joyful symbol of hope and renewal.

The Ark came to rest finally on Mt. Ararat and Noah ordered the great doors of gopher wood to be opened.

The animals streamed out into the sunshine and raced into the woods and down the mountainside to the pastures below.

'And what do we do now?' asked Naamah?

'The first thing I'm going to do is to open a winery,' said Noah.

'But you need grapes to make wine,' replied his wife.

'You're right, as usual, my dear. So, the first thing I'm going to do is to plant a vineyard.'

That is exactly what he did.

And that, children, is how we were blessed with wine.

A Final Thought

If this goes on much longer, I'll be able to see my grandchildren through university on the refunds from empty wine bottles. **RP**.

About The Author

Tony Aspler is an internationally known writer, speaker, and wine expert, based in St. Catharines, Ontario. He has been writing about wine for over 40 years. He was the wine columnist for The Toronto Star for 21 years and has authored nineteen books on wine and food, including *The Wine Atlas of Canada*, *Vintage Canada*, *The Wine Lover's Companion*, *The Wine Lover Cooks*, *Travels with My Corkscrew* and *Tony Aspler's Cellar Book*. Tony's latest book is *Five Minutes More*, a sequel to *The Five-Minute Wine Book*.

He is the author and co-author of ten novels, including four with Gordon Pape: *Chain Reaction*, *The Scorpion Sanction*, *The Music Wars*, and the soon-to-be published, *A Taste of Evil*.

His latest series is a collection of wine murder mysteries featuring the itinerant wine writer/detective Ezra Brant: *Blood Is Thicker than Beaujolais*, *The Beast of Barbaresco* and *Death on the Douro*. *Nightmare in Napa* is to be published next year.

Tony wrote two half-hour episodes for the CBC-TV historical series *The Campbells*, and co-wrote with Gordon Pape an hour-long radio adaptation of their novel *Chain Reaction*.

In December 2007, Tony was awarded the Order of Canada.

In 2012 Tony was the first Canadian to be inducted into the New York Media Wine Writers Hall of Fame. He was awarded the Queen's Jubilee Medal. In 2017 Tony was awarded Spain's Officers Cross of the Order of Civil Merit.

In February 2001, Tony co-founded a charitable foundation with Arlene Willis, Grapes for Humanity (www.grapesforhumanity.com).

Tony Aspler's website can be found at **www.tonyaspler.com**.